# It Can Happen Today!

# It Can Happen Today!

Principles of Church Growth
from the Book of Acts

## G. Edwin Bontrager
## and Nathan D. Showalter

Foreword by C. Peter Wagner

HERALD PRESS
Scottdale, Pennsylvania
Kitchener, Ontario
1986

**Library of Congress Cataloging-in-Publication Data**
Bontrager, G. Edwin, 1939-
    It can happen today!

    1. Bible. N.T.    Acts—Criticism, interpretation,
etc.    2.  Church growth—Biblical teaching.
I.  Showalter, Nathan D., 1949-              II.  Title.
BS2625.2.B64 1986              254'.5              86-15036
ISBN 0-8361-3419-2 (pbk.)

IT CAN HAPPEN TODAY!
Copyright © 1986 by Herald Press, Scottdale, Pa.  15683
        Published simultaneously in Canada by Herald Press,
        Kitchener, Ont.  N2G 4M5. All rights reserved.
Library of Congress Catalog Card Number: 86-15036
International Standard Book Number: 0-8361-3419-2
Printed in the United States of America
Design by Gwen M. Stamm

86 87 88 89 90 91 9 8 7 6 5 4 3 2 1

# Contents

# Foreword

This book is the first of a kind. I suppose that if all the commentaries published on the book of Acts were gathered together, they would comprise a small library. But none of them would do what Edwin Bontrager and Nathan Showalter have done. They have succeeded in making the principles of church growth which operated in the first century come alive for churches today.

Much writing in the field of church growth is sociologically based with scant reference to the Word of God. This book is different. It begins with careful studies of thirteen church growth dynamics in the book of Acts and then shows how each one can apply to your church today. It combines sound theory with an amazing practicality.

*It Can Happen Today!* is written in plain English. One does not have to be a scholar to understand it. But it is not simplistic. It will stimulate keen minds and inspire warm hearts to move out into the community with the good news of Jesus Christ. It is a book for all Christians to enjoy and to apply.

The title is well chosen. It *can* happen today. We know it can because church growth even in much more dramatic form than we read about in the book of Acts is now happening in many parts of the world.

Is it happening in your community? In your

church? If not, read this book. Distribute it among your church members. Teach it in your adult Sunday school classes. Pray that God will burn its message into your hearts. And then act. Move out in the power of the Holy Spirit as the believers did in Jerusalem, Judea, and to the uttermost parts of the earth.

If you do, it *will* happen today!

—*C. Peter Wagner*
*Fuller Theological Seminary*
*Pasadena, California*

# Authors' Preface

Twenty centuries later we are still trying to learn about the dynamic that caused the phenomenal growth in the early church. From 120 people to multitudes of Christians—from one small fellowship to a multiplication of churches—Christianity spread. At first we hear of Peter, Philip, and Paul, among others, who introduced Jesus to the Roman world. But during the great age of expansion that followed Paul, we do not hear the name of a single outstanding missionary. The work was done instead by countless obscure men and women who shared this good news within their own circles of friends and relatives.

Can it happen today? Can congregations composed of redeemed believers who hold as so important the way of the Christian faith find a way to penetrate their neighborhoods? Churches which catch the message and methods and excitement of those early Christians can do none other than grow. A lay leader in one denomination was heard to say, "We want to let our light shine. We hope that people will see us and a few will join." But the believers in Acts certainly did not take that kind of passive approach. Mission was the driving force of the church, not an added-on sideline that was engaged in if time permitted or if it was easy.

Today's churches that wish to effectively reach out cannot depend on their "welcome" sign to bring people in, while they pour countless hours into the maintenance of their organization.

This book is a deductive study of Acts, highlighting events and strategies that served to move the church in mission. The themes that will provide insight are community life, prayer, leadership, personal witness, prayer, church planting, unity, restriction, and persecution. If today's local church wishes to be faithful in mission and yearns to help seek and save the lost, it will need to adopt a balance of all that happened in the early church.

Thirteen themes are developed in *It Can Happen Today!* Each chapter presents a study of the chosen Scripture passage, followed by an application and challenge to the church today. A companion teacher's manual is available for use with this book.

We hope and pray that as you read these insights and apply these principles from Acts, you and the people in your church will see by experience that mission certainly can happen today!

—*G. Edwin Bontrager*
*Nathan D. Showalter*

# It Can Happen Today!

# 1

# Power to Grow

*Acts 1:1-14*

## Getting Started

If a congregation wants to reach out and grow, it will need power. Where will that power come from? We Americans are enamored with financial power and military power. But we experience a dearth of spiritual power. Though the community of faith goes through the exercises of religion, it ends up many times with a stunted power supply. Without energy there is no growth.

## Echoes from the Upper Room

The curtain opens. Before us lies the book of Acts, a story begun by Luke in his Gospel. We see on the stage a young group of disciples, some of whom have had three years with Jesus. As the drama begins, we see them in a fellowship huddle, waiting. They are waiting for power. Jesus had said, "But you will receive power when the Holy Spirit comes on you; and you will be my witnesses in Jerusalem, and in all Judea and Samaria, and to the ends of the earth" (Acts 1:8).

They no longer have the everyday contact with Jesus like they had before his death. He is still alive—that much is clear. But he is not to be any longer living with them, traveling with them, eating with them, and teaching them. How, then, are they to maintain their sense of pur-

13

pose and direction as disciples of Jesus?

The new movement faces a crucial test. It must grow, even in the absence of Jesus' physical presence with them, or it will fall apart. What kind of power do they need? Where will the disciples find the power to grow?

Through the Holy Spirit they were to find the continued power of their Lord's companionship. The power they were receiving found its basis in that which Jesus had left with them—the power of his words and deeds. Jesus was a teacher whose actions matched his words. He practiced what he preached.

The authority of his teaching was related to the powerful reinforcement which his deeds brought to his words. He did not throw out a range of options, several theories, or kaleidoscopic speculations. Jesus gave "commandment through the Holy Spirit." His was a decisive word, not the take-it-or-leave-it scholarship of the scribes.

Jesus was about to replace the disciples' old nature, which was too weary and tired to change dramatically, to a new nature. Their mistrust, doubt, and discouragement would be replaced by faith, hope, and love.

This new power out of which the growth of the church would proceed, though rooted in Jesus' example, would be borne along through an implantation of an entirely new life and motive for living, empowered by the Holy Spirit.

These early followers received this Spirit power because they took their Christian commitment seriously. And in their commitment they discovered the following "power principles."

1. *They heard the commandment that Jesus gave* (vv. 2-3).

The disciples had always been listening to Jesus during those three years, but sometimes they were not hearing. Now since the resurrection they listened in rapt attention because they knew Jesus would soon be gone.

Throughout the forty days from the resurrection to ascension, Jesus impressed upon them that what happens in mission depends upon them. Verse 3b says, "He appeared to them over a period of forty days and spoke about the kingdom of God." They were being briefed and challenged. Their evangelism thrust throughout the book of Acts proved that they had *heard*. There is power in hearing.

2. *They met together* (vv. 6, 13-14).

Meeting together provided opportunities for these disciples to remind each other of the Lord's words. Probably no one had accurately recorded them in scroll form.

Their commonality around Jesus drew them together. Their sincere desire for fellowship and nurture gave the impetus for their encounters with each other. The upper room experience was only a beginning. Home cells played a vital part in the life and growth of the church.

3. *They waited for the promise of the Father* (v. 4).

Drawing their strength from one another they waited patiently for the gift which "my Father promised, which you have heard me speak about" (v. 4). Jesus knew they would gain more power and courage if they would be willing to wait for a time.

Their minds possibly went back to those poignant words from Isaiah, "They that wait upon the Lord shall renew their strength" (Isa. 40:31 KJV). Strength for mission and growth came about through silence, contemplation, meditation, and prayer.

There is power in waiting.

4. *They desired power* (v. 6).

"Power" was a keyword of the day. The Romans now had power. Would Israel regain their right to self-rule?

15

James and John had asked Jesus earlier if they would be able to sit on the right and left sides of him when he set up his kingdom. Now they asked again (probably with ulterior motives) if this was the time for Israel to ascend to power.

Jesus exclaimed to them that they will not only see the power of God displayed through them in Israel, but also to Samaria, and to the ends of the earth (note 1:8). Obviously this was a different kind of power, one that grabbed them and wouldn't let them go. It was a creative, freeing power, not a dominating, controlling one. Thus, they began to release their desire for coercive power as they experienced the power of Jesus.

Power can come, but only through a keen desire for it.

### 5. *They prayed* (v. 14).

With the ascension, Jesus was physically gone. Conversation with him was no longer possible. Yet talking to him continued through the medium of prayer. The disciples "joined together constantly in prayer...."

We should note that in Luke 3:21 Jesus was praying before the descent of the Spirit on him. In v. 14 the apostles and their companions were praying before the Holy Spirit made his descent upon them. Luke seems to repeat the idea that one of the objects of prayer is the request for the gift of the Spirit.

There is power in prayer.

### 6. *They were unified* (v. 14).

In the minds of the 120 disciples in the upper room, Jesus and his purpose for them came first. They were unified around that. All else was second. This enabled them to spend ten full days together. Power for evangelism was a direct outcome.

There is power in being unified around one common goal.

16

## In Your Hometown

The church today can know the same power for which the disciples waited, the same spiritual power which distinguished Jesus' teaching from that of the religious intellectuals. It is the power of the Holy Spirit which changes word into Word, theory into commandment, option into mandate, speculation into commission. In the school of the Holy Spirit, words become more than a medium of dialogue. They become authoritative directives in God's new administration. Words, when empowered by the Spirit, are not a passive substance for our human manipulation. They are rather the rigorous messengers of good news.

Has your congregation experienced this power? Have you returned to Jerusalem to wait for God to act? Or are you sitting hopelessly, aimlessly in Galilee?

What provides the power for the risen Savior's work in your church and community? Sometimes people focus on a traditionalism as the enabling force for church ministry. Others find family cohesiveness as their power source. For some, carrying on a denominational image provides a source of energy. These all have some validity, but how long can a church exist only on these? A greater power is imperative if a church is to be effective for witness, growth, and endurance.

## Decision

As you think about the energizing sources available, try to determine which two or three of the six "power principles" would help activate a weakness in your church. How could you, with the Holy Spirit's help, bring about new life and vitality if you would work on those items and incorporate them as priorities for the next six months?

# 2

# The New Community Established

*Acts 2:37-47*

## Getting Started

Community—what is it? Community is people coming together, people being united around a cause, an idea, a leader, a shared culture, or even a task. Communities, like persons, are born, go through infancy, adolescence, and mid-life crises. And they sometimes become senile and die.

As you witness the birth of a new community and its continued growth in this lesson, reflect on your own congregation. How does it compare? Where are you in the life stages of congregations?

## Turning Around on Jerusalem's Street

1. *Repentance.* The key impetus for this new community was repentance. This coming together required a turning from other competing loyalties. It is difficult to imagine the variegated colors and backgrounds of those thousands of people amassed together on Jerusalem's streets. But no matter what their traditional Judaic beliefs, they were "cut to the heart" and said, "Brothers, what shall we do?" (2:37) At that point 3,000 people who had gathered into an auditorium of streets and open windows around the upper room made a U-turn—they changed their minds, and turned to Jesus. That funda-

mental change in direction is what the Bible calls "repentance."

A person who is walking down the street in one direction is not likely to turn around and start walking the other direction unless she gets a message, unless she hears, either from within or without, a word that changes her mind.

That word came on Pentecost from Peter, the preacher. Peter unashamedly and without fear of the authorities became a messenger through whom God worked to bring about the establishment of his new community.

2. *Baptism.* Baptism is a public sign of repentance and identification with the new community. Because it is such an important ceremony, it is not surprising to discover that Christians have often disagreed as to its meaning and practice.

In Acts 2, however, we have the first post-Pentecostal baptism, without even a hint of controversy. The baptism tradition of John was simply carried into the Spirit-filled community as a sign of faith and obedience, death and new life. It was an "initiation" rite for the 3,000 who were that day reborn. But controversy will come soon enough to the fledgling fellowship.

3. *Community.* Acts 2:42-43 gives us five vital signs of new community life:
    1. Bible-centered teaching
    2. Spirit-filled fellowship
    3. Ministering to needs (breaking of bread)
    4. Prayer
    5. Witness (everyone was filled with awe)

Signs and wonders were common in the community. The power of symbol and miracle is often witnessed in a fresh movement of God's Spirit. We read about this power throughout the New Testament.

## On the Street Where You Live

Do you find your neighbors clamoring for an answer to "How can I be saved?" Probably not. At least, not outwardly. But many people inwardly are looking for answers to those innate fears and yearnings. People in your community who seem self-sufficient and who seem to have it all together are crying out for an inner assurance that will see them through all the uncertainties of life and death.

In a recent study by George Gallup, Jr., and David Poling, released in the book entitled *The Search for America's Faith*, it was discovered that 61 million American adults are not members of any church or religious institution. That is 41 percent of the adult population. Half of the unchurched respondents said they could foresee the possibility of a situation in the future where they might "become a fairly active member" of a church or synagogue.

The call that comes to our congregations today is to take the challenge to seek and save those who are lost. We are the "Peters" today—evangelists (persons who share the good news about Jesus). We are his witnesses. The New Testament word of "witness" is the word from which we derive our modern word "martyr."

"When the people *heard* this" (2:37), they were ready to repent. The lack of repentance in our lives, and in the lives of non-Christians around us, is often related to the absence of the Word. But when the Word was preached, the Lord added to their number.

"How, then, can they call on the one they have not believed in? And how can they believe in the one of whom they have not heard? And how can they hear without someone preaching to them? And how can they preach unless they are sent?" (Romans 10:14-15).

The imperative comes to us who have heard to search out those unchurched persons who are looking for a community of faith, some of whom may live on your street. Though you may not be a preacher as Peter was, you can creatively find ways to bring about repentance, which can lead through God's power to new life and even baptism within your church.

The effective communication of God's Word— whether through preaching, personal witness, or in deeds of love and justice—is the foundation of the church. Only by understanding God's Word can people truly repent, receive Christ, and through the Holy Spirit, be baptized and brought into the new community.

Baptism is one of the first and most important steps in a life of faithfulness following the new birth.

Some of the new believers may have been baptized earlier under the baptism of John. But now they were being baptized *in the name of Jesus.* They were declaring their allegiance to the Messiah and to his kingdom.

Look again at the five vital signs of new community life (Acts 2:42-43). Are those the marks of your church? Are you effective in attracting new believers in this way?

Congregations today can move out in the power of the Spirit, ministering to the needs of their communities, bringing persons to repentance and baptism. But to covet the power to do wonders and miraculous signs without commitment to a disciplined new community life described by these five vital signs will only issue in frustration and defeat.

The new community, made up of Christians living in harmony with God's purpose, will demonstrate signs of spiritual power in witness and service. Emil Brunner set forth this maxim, "The church exists by mission as a fire exists by burning." It can happen today!

## Decision

As you think about the vital signs of the new community, try to determine which of these five are strengths of your church and which are weaknesses. List them one to five from strongest to weakest. What can you do to make the weak stronger?

# 3

# Leadership and Cultural Diversity

*Acts 6:1-7*

## Getting started

The number of disciples was increasing by the hundreds. Many people were leaving their own way of life and were discovering the new. But this rapid growth evoked a crisis in the early church. Because of the apostles' "community sharing" concept, a complaint arose that discrimination was taking place in the distribution of goods.

"Something is going wrong!" they exclaimed. The problem proved to be a turning point for the new community. A whole new corps of leadership emerged.

## Visiting the Apostles' Church Board

As we sit in on the apostles' church board, we note that the call to come to Christ was open to all, not only Palestinian Jews. Grecian Jews as well were becoming believers. These Grecian Jews had most likely come to Jerusalem from foreign countries for Pentecost, had discovered this new life in Christ, and had remained. They could not speak Aramaic as the "home" Jews could. It seemed like the spiritually snobbish Aramaic-speaking Jews despised these "foreigners." Therefore the alms which were to be divided out evenly among all widows were not shared with these "foreigners."

23

Now they were meeting to ask the question, "What shall we do?" After some serious deliberations, the decision was reached to appoint a team of workers who would see to it that the distribution of food be done properly— that equity would be a priority. Seven men were selected to perform this practical service so that the twelve apostles could continue in the ministry of the Word and in prayer.

Most likely all but one of the seven "deacons," as they have been called, were native-born Jews, although according to their names, some were themselves Grecian Jews. Nicolas had been a Gentile who had embraced the Jewish faith.

The varied backgrounds of these men was a key factor in their success. Each could direct his efforts to the needs he could best fill. And because of the proper use of their gifts, the problem was solved and equity reigned.

Now look at the results. By not allowing this problem to fester and grow, the apostles cared for the disciples on the home front, causing the church to reach out even more. The number of disciples in Jerusalem increased rapidly. The message of the cross struck at the hearts of a great multitude of priests. Most likely these priests had opposed the gospel more than any other class of Jews had. But the power of truth won them over.

## Meanwhile, Back to Your Church Board

When churches today find an influx of new persons within their fellowships, a similar situation can develop. If we would sit in on a church board or leadership team today facing this challenge, what would be said? How would it be handled?

If our churches are to grow, we will need more leaders. The pastor will not have the time to minister to all the new people the church has the potential of reaching. Furthermore, the present leaders may be more in tune with maintenance ministry than with mission ministry. They may not have the gifts nor the time for "frontline" outreach ministries.

Therefore leadership drawn from outside the inner circle is an important asset. The seven chosen were apparently tested and proven, but had not been on the "church board" before.

Newly chosen leadership people should be delegated responsibility along with a task. They should not feel restrained in their ministry, but should be carrying out the overall purpose of the sending body, accountable to it. Stephen and Philip became evangelists. Tradition says that Prochorus later assisted John and then became a bishop and a martyr.

If the basic leadership group keeps church growth as its overall goal, those individuals or groups who push out in evangelistic efforts will not need to circumvent the organizational procedures in the church. By taking this approach, their ministries will be looked upon as more credible.

For the local church to grow today, the base of leadership in the congregation needs to be expanded. There are two models of leadership. In one model, new programs and ministries are continually initiated with one leader trying to oversee all of them. This approach may have very negative results. In fact, either the ministries will suffer, or the leader will drown in all the work.

In the other model, new leaders are developed as new ministries are added. New leadership, carefully chosen, thoroughly counseled, and adequately trained, can give a strong base to new programs.

When we choose leaders we must be careful about the ones who always say "Yes." They can easily become overloaded with all kinds of unrelated tasks, while another person stands by with nothing to do. Leadership distribution is imperative to the growing church.

We need a variety of leaders with different gifts. In the early church each of these seven chosen had his own unique gift of leadership—some directed to ministries within, and others to witness without. Today in our culture, we find both men *and* women who can offer their gifts.

In this early growing church, leadership was chosen, commissioned, and delegated responsibility. The apostles could then spend their time in prayer, in study, and in teaching the Word. The teaching continued to provide the impetus for this kind of social action—the distribution of alms—as well as continual evangelism by these deacons and the other Christians.

## Decision

Throughout the Bible we find sheep used as a symbol for God's people today. Sheep do not take care of themselves. They require much attention. This is especially true of young lambs, which in biblical imagery refers to new Christians among us.

What can you do to make certain that leadership is being provided for those who will come into your sheepfold? Is leadership being spread out in your congregation? You may wish to examine your nominating and selection system. How can your church provide solid training for potential leaders? Is your congregation ready to put its trust in newer leaders? Remember that new members in your church may have God-given leadership gifts.

# 4

# Personal Witnessing

*Acts 8:26-40*

## Getting Started

Before Pentecost Jesus told his followers, "When the Holy Spirit comes, you will be witnesses." Witnessing is not optional; it is an essential quality of discipleship. The word "witness" is not only what the Christian does verbally, but also what the Christian is as a person. This account from Philip's ministry concentrates on the verbal aspects of witness. This is what we find most difficult to do. But it is essential if the church is to grow and God's lost children are to be found.

## Bumping Along in a Chariot

Philip's sensitivity to the Spirit's leading, his gentleness and polite inquisitiveness, his clear and concise explanation of the Word, and his ability to clarify commitment were all part of what made Philip an effective witness. He had an overall goal in mind—to lead this Ethiopian man to commitment and baptism—but he did it without violating the official's own personality. There was no force used; the events and words used from the initial contact to the final farewell all flowed naturally. There was no need for Philip to be nervous or feel inhibited. He sensed a need and with the Spirit's help, he met that need.

Let us look at these marks of an effective witness.

1. *Philip listened to the Spirit* (Acts 6:5; 8:26, 29, 39).

Philip was an effective witness because he was in constant conversation with the Holy Spirit. He was originally called to leadership in the church because he was "full of faith and of the Holy Spirit" (Acts 6:5). He was ready to leave the excitement of the revival going on in Samaria and head out into the wilderness, because he heard the heavenly voice. It was the voice of the Spirit that prompted Philip to initiate the conversation with this lone traveling foreigner.

The Holy Spirit today can and will prepare our way for witness when we are wholly given over to his plan for us. We can witness effectively as we are guided by the Spirit.

2. *Philip was inquisitive* (Acts 8:30).

Philip could have begun the conversation with the Ethiopian official by giving a mini-sermon about Jesus and about the revival going on in Samaria. After all, he was under divine instruction to approach this particular individual. But he did not begin that way. He began with a question: "Do you understand what you are reading?"

Spirit-filled witnesses are always inquisitive, always good listeners. They want to discover what the Spirit has already done in the lives of other people. They want to work with the Spirit in sharing the good news about Jesus, building on the foundation already laid. A Spirit-filled witness assumes that God has already planted a seed of interest or understanding in the person's heart, and that her work is to water that seed and nurture the fragile seedling.

Effective witnesses learn how to ask provocative questions—questions that encourage the seeker to describe his search, to own his need, to knock on the door of understanding that the witness stands ready to open.

3. *Philip knew the Word* (Acts 8:35).

Philip did not ask questions or listen because he was ignorant, but because he knew the ways of the Spirit who "blows where he wills" (John 3:8). Philip not only knew the Spirit; he also knew the Word.

Philip began with that very passage of Scripture and told him the good news about Jesus. He did not have a previously prepared outline of the gospel. He began with the question that the Ethiopian raised (Acts 8:34) and went from there to explain the good news about Jesus.

Most likely Philip had previously learned a systematic approach to sharing the gospel. No doubt while preaching in his "Samaritan Crusade," Philip had followed a previously thought-out plan, as did Peter and Paul when they preached and taught. Having this basic knowledge of the gospel message allowed this messenger of God for this particular occasion, bumping along in a chariot, to tap into his knowledge at the point where this struggling seeker could find satisfactory answers.

We cannot share God's Word if we do not know it ourselves. We cannot explain the way of salvation if we are not sure that we understand it clearly.

4. *Philip knew how to clarify commitment* (Acts 8:38).

Philip again shows his effectiveness as a witness by combining all three qualities of Spirit-filled witness; he listened to the Spirit, he listened to what the Ethiopian was thinking and saying, and he acted in obedience to the Word. In combining those three actions, he was able to lead this Ethiopian official to commit his life to Jesus and be baptized.

Most encounters are not this easy. In this case, the seeker appealed to the one witnessing to seal his commitment with baptism. Philip, wishing to be sure that the Ethiopian was aware that baptism was not in and of itself the key to salvation in the seeker's mind, inquired further regarding his confession of faith. "I believe that Jesus Christ is the Son of God," exclaimed the official. And upon coming to an oasis in the desert, he was baptized.

It is difficult for the person witnessing to know when a seeker is ready to make that commitment. Christians many times refrain from witnessing because they think they need to see a resulting conversion, and therefore fear that the seeker will "turn them down." As we grow in our maturity as witnesses, we will be able to discern where a person is in her search for God. Sometimes we will share words that will cause serious thought, but not a full commitment. Sometimes we will have the joy of walking with the person the final steps to the cross.

## What About Divine Appointments Today?

Should you wait to witness until the Spirit picks you up and carries you to that person totally prepared to listen and respond? Optimum conditions and optimum times for witness come few and far between. To be effective witnesses, you must be sensitive to the Spirit. Still, your humanness will tell you that you are not quite prepared, or the time is not quite right.

You need to remember that witnesses are qualified not by their speaking ability or by their communication techniques, but by having seen the event under consideration. Jesus' disciples were witnesses because of what they had seen—because they had been with Jesus, not because they had taken an evangelism seminar or attended an evangelical college.

Are you a qualified witness? It is true that we have not seen Jesus nor his deeds of power personally. Nor have we heard his authoritative word of good news. But if we have a personal relationship with him, then we are witnesses.

Besides this personal experience with Christ which qualifies us as witnesses, we also have the power of the Holy Spirit in our lives as we are obedient to him. Jesus said that the Spirit's presence in our lives is so important that we have the potential to do even greater things than he did (John 14).

Your commitment to Christ and your knowledge that all people are eternally lost without Christ will motivate you to be a witness—a verbal witness. Being a witness through living out a good life is certainly basic, but before your unsaved friends will make a change, they need to hear from you verbally what has happened in your life.

## Decision

Will you be a witness? You may say, "I try to witness, but my words are so faltering, so clumsy." But consider this: No one ever learned to walk without stumbling at first. The key is persistence. The motivation is love. Even faltering words are powerful tools when the Spirit is at work. "When I am weak," wrote the great missionary Paul, "then I am strong!"

This strength in weakness can happen to you today!

# 5

# Conversion and Church Growth

*Acts 9:1-19*

## Getting Started

"Born again" has become a popular phrase in recent years. Even though it is biblically based, the concept has met with misinterpretation and misunderstanding. What, then, do we understand it to mean? "Born again" in its traditional Christian use does not imply just a remodeling job or a self-imposed renewal of one's inner life. It is a spiritual transformation from inside out reflected in one's life.

Biblical "conversion" is more than a face lift, a dieting plan, or an academic degree, though humanly speaking these have brought about physical and mental changes to people. The "conversion" in Acts 9 pictures Paul setting out in a new direction. The deep recesses of Paul's inner self were renewed by the hand of God. Conversion is turning from sin and turning to God, being re-created by the Creator. It is symbolized in baptism and is sustained in the new community.

## Steps Taken on the Road to Damascus

What a different man Paul was when he left this Syrian city a few days later! He had left Jerusalem as leader of a "death squad." But by the time he got to Damascus, he was ready to accept the faith he had come

33

to stamp out. Obviously something had happened. A change so dramatic and so sudden can only be attributed to God's Spirit who had already been at work in the life of this colorful character, Paul.

The steps from antagonism to acceptance and conversion are clearly visible in this short narrative. As you look at these steps in Paul's experience, you may become more aware that persons around you whom you wish to lead to conversion are at various stages also. If you want your church to grow, it is imperative that you sense the levels or stages to which people have arrived. Then you can lead them further in concert with the Holy Spirit to conversion and baptism, and then to growth and reproduction.

Note briefly these steps in Saul's adventure.

### 1. Saul had become aware of God.

Saul was a "God-fearer." He had grown up in a strict Jewish home, had learned about the Lord, and had taken upon himself the requirements of the law, including the Pharisaical code (Phil. 3:4-6). He knew what God expected from the Jews. He was determined to carry out those expectations and not allow any Jews to be persuaded otherwise. Even his opposition to the new Christian communities grew out of his zeal for God. Paul tells us later that his persecution of the church was part of his misguided efforts to obey God.

### 2. Saul accepted Christ.

In Acts 22:10 (a parallel passage to our text pertaining to Saul's conversion) he exclaimed, "What shall I do, Lord?" Though his past was being judged and his vision of persecuting Christians was being challenged, he had no problem in following instructions that would catapult him into an altogether new way of thinking. That is the essence of conversion—leaving the old and accepting the new.

*3. Saul repented and set a new direction for his life.*

Struck down in blindness, he was led by the hand to Damascus, as one would lead a child. When Ananias found him, he found a broken, contrite, praying disciple instead of a shrewd, dogmatic, and vicious persecutor. Saul, no doubt, had already repented of his blindness of spirit before Ananias came to counsel him. His praying had included a humble request for forgiveness of sins and an invitation for the Spirit of Jesus to infill his life and being.

*4. Saul made public his decision.*

Though hesitant at first to meet Saul, Ananias, a God-fearing man, went to find him. Next, Saul evaluated his experience with help from Ananias. In his decision to be baptized as a new believer, he was sealing his decision, thus opening for himself a new course for life. His conversion evoked within him a desire to strike out in an altogether new direction.

*5. Saul made contact with other believers.*

Saul, along with his spiritual mentor, Ananias, realized that a conversion without contact with other disciples could be disastrous. He was already being incorporated into fellowship (9:19b). The disciples, although at first hesitant, rallied around him, proving their trust and discovering Saul's trustworthiness.

*6. Saul became a disciple, a learner.*

After conversion must come growth. Paul spent three years in Damascus and Arabia in study, reflection, and preaching—all the time building a solid foundation for his missionary enterprise. His first missionary journey began ten years later. However, his missionary message began immediately. As he grew, he shared. The ebb and flow of his ministry, his receiving and giving, built him into the kind of solid, courageous, and effective missionary he was. True conversion results in the discovery and use of spiritual gifts, a dependence on prayer, and the reproducing of other Christians.

## Flashes of Light Today

To help our churches grow today, we must continue to see a steady stream of conversions. Many congregations wonder if "outsiders" can fit into a new pattern of life. You may wonder whether you should pursue efforts to reach your lost neighbors because you question if they can make the switch and live upright lives equal to yours. In fact, that may be the same question your lost neighbor is asking.

But we must put priorities in the right place. Let us lead them to Christ and then trust the Spirit's work. As churches in mission, we must be winning persons, leading them to conversion through Christ our communities of faith. If we are not, we must question whether our Christian faith is valid even for ourselves and our own children. A credible and workable Christian faith will be a reproducing faith. Otherwise, it is only a cultural practice, or a localized moral code.

But your non-Christian neighbors are at different points in their "Damascus roads." Some have not yet begun. What do these persons think about Christianity? If you inquire, you will discover some with little knowledge of God. Others may know the Bible quite well. Some may feel guilty because of the way they are living, while others seem to have little awareness of sin. Some, like Saul, are doing the wrong things for the right reasons, while others are doing the right things for the wrong reasons.

Research has shown that the unchurched are most responsive during periods of transition in their lives. The most important of these transitions include: (1) the death of a spouse, (2) divorce, (3) marital separation, (4) a jail term, (5) the death of a close family member. If you wish to reach your neighbors, you need to relate and witness to them during these and other times of significant change.

Young people are naturally receptive to information which makes sense and fills their needs. Valid conversion among youth is important. It is said that 85 percent will not receive Christ after the age of 18, and only one out of 15,000 will be converted after the age of 65.

Can conversions be different for different people? Some persons can point to a certain time and place for their conversion. Others know they have received Christ, but cannot pinpoint particulars. Their experience could be called a "growth in grace." Experiencing a crisis experience may have one advantage. In such a crisis, a person may have an emotional experience of ecstasy, which, though short-lived, may chart a new course for life. And throughout life a passion is lived out that was born in one brief moment.

Biblical conversions, however, were not all identical. We do not know for sure when Saul's took place. The flash of light was an attention-getter. In Acts 9:11 Saul was praying. No doubt, he was entreating God for forgiveness of sins.

Conversion came as a result of faith in Christ. When the Lord spoke to Ananias (vv. 11-12, 15-16), he made no comment about Saul's past. The Lord's words intimated that Saul accepted him by faith alone. Though hate had been brewing in Saul's heart against Christians, yet Ananias must have believed that Saul had already changed before Ananias personally met him. Just as works will not save us, so works that we have done before will not keep from saving us.

Note that Saul was nurtured and accepted into the community of believers by a concerted effort on their part. Ananias placed great trust in Saul, as we noted (v. 17). Saul spent several days with the Damascus disciples (v. 19b). No doubt they established Saul in the truth about the Messiah who fulfilled the Old Testament law. Those first few days showed that the disciples trusted and loved Saul. Learning about this love implanted a deep love in Saul for those yet unconverted.

## Decision

For your church to experience steady growth it is important that you find ways of assimilating those new disciples within your community of faith.

Are there "Sauls" who live near you whom you feel at times are beyond reclamation? Faith can overcome fear as you make efforts to go to them. If a person is living in corrupt waywardness, but expresses a desire to change, ask her to have a simple faith in Christ for salvation. What opportunities do you see for such witness? Make it a matter of prayer. How can one assist a person to act in newness of life after conversion while showing grace and love?

The grace of God can change today's Sauls. It certainly can happen today!

# 6

# Good News for All

*Acts 10:1-48*

## Getting Started

Up to this time in the early church, the gospel had been contained among the Jews. But such good news had to leak out sooner or later. A centurion from Caesarea was about to be the first Gentile to become part of the new community.

Had not Jesus predicted such a bridging of the good news? This Caesarean soldier was not the first centurion who made known his need for Jesus. We encounter the first in Matthew 8. This man's faith had so impressed Jesus that he exclaimed,

> I tell you the truth, I have not found anyone in Israel with such great faith! I say to you that many will come from the east and the west, and will take their places at the feast with Abraham, Isaac and Jacob in the kingdom of heaven (Matt. 8:10-11).

This prophetic word was about to be fulfilled. Jesus had reached out, even if reluctantly, to Gentile seekers (see Mark 7:24-30), but the good news since Pentecost had been preached only to the Jewish audience. So God decided to use more extreme measures to get the point across: the good news was meant for all!

## Visions by the Sea

Both Cornelius, a God-fearing Gentile, and Peter, a staunch and traditional Jew, were to be changed because of special messages by God in two visions. Cornelius saw the vision of an angel in the seacoast city of Caesarea, a Roman city and official residence both of Herodian kings and the Roman procurators. It was distinctly Gentile.

Peter saw his "sheet vision" (10:11) in Joppa, forty miles to the south. A seaport city serving Jerusalem, Joppa was clearly Jewish since 40 B.C. when it was taken from the Syrians and given to the Jews. The two visions in these two contrasting villages by the sea were to change the course of the Christian church.

Peter could not have known just how much his comfortable Jewish world would be turned upside down by some noontime prayers in Joppa. The Jews believed in things "kosher." But what is "kosher"?

The Jews had strict food laws. Generally speaking, the Jew might eat only animals which chewed the cud and whose hoofs were split. All others were unclean and forbidden. These commands, based in Leviticus 11, contrasted with this vision by the sea and left Peter rather confused. Three times Peter was asked to kill and eat. (God seemed to deal with Peter in threes. We remember that three times the Lord said to him, "You will deny me." And three times he was asked by Jesus, "Do you love me?")

But as this vision was beginning to register, Peter was becoming prepared for these nonkosher Gentiles who were knocking on his front door. After all, Peter was staying with Simon the tanner, who in his occupation worked with the unkosher skins of dead animals. It seems as though the barriers were breaking down. And now here they were—these men seeking after him. One wonders whether Peter had all these thoughts sorted out in his mind when he gave in to the coaxing of these men and began that journey to Caesarea.

Now the good news would be preached to Greek-speaking Gentiles, people who feared God, but who did not follow the law of Moses. Peter introduced his sermon to the gathering in the centurion's house with these historic words:

> I now realize how true it is that God does not show favoritism but accepts men from every nation who fear him and do what is right (Acts 10:34-35).

Paul indicated in Romans 1:16 that though the gospel had been for the Jew first, it was now for the Gentiles as well. Romans 2:9-11 says that God does not show favoritism. James speaks of favoritism toward the wealthy (James 2:1ff.). The ushers of the congregation were showing the well-dressed persons to the best seats, while the poor were asked to stand or sit on a footstool. Such discrimination is sharply condemned in the Bible.

But the favoritism for which Peter had been rebuked was of a different sort. It was a deeper, more subtle kind of discrimination. Rather than being based on wealth or class, it was based on race. The issue that the Spirit dealt with here was a kind of spiritual racism that limited God's grace to Jewish people. Gentiles, like Cornelius, could only be saved, in effect, by becoming Jews.

But no longer! The good news is now for all. God had indeed chosen the Jews, but he chose them to bring light to the nations. No longer would the light be hidden under a kosher basket. The community of Jesus would be a city set on a hill, and its glory would be seen by Gentiles and Jews alike, uneducated as well as educated, slave and free.

## How Large Is Your Vision?

It is a blight on the Christian church today that many congregations of believers scattered across our country retreat to their little Joppas, strongholds of a particular set of doctrines. There they are satisfied and there they pray. Peter felt comfortable going up on the flat rooftop, undisturbed and unhindered, overlooking the beautiful Mediterranean for prayer. But he felt a little more anxious, and possibly a bit troubled, taking that large step which took the Jewish church "across the tracks" to Gentile Caesarea.

As we gather in our congregations for singing, worship, instruction, fellowship, and shepherding, the Lord asks that we increase our vision for those "Gentiles" yet unreached. Those "Gentiles" may be those whom we are calling "common" or "unclean." But are they really? They may be different than we, but are they not also part of the world for whom Christ died? Cultural differences do exist. People come from varied traditions and backgrounds. They may live in another part of town. But they are in need of the message of Christ just as was Cornelius and his household.

So where shall we look to find "Cornelius"? In thinking about evangelism both at home and abroad, we sometimes talk about four levels of communication with regard to cultural difference. As we examine each of these, try to think about what you and your church could do to cause the good news to leap the barriers which keep you from evangelizing these groups of people. We need to discover with Peter that the lost are not all dirty and unclean and self-satisfied. Some are just out of our evangelistic line of sight. With Peter we may come to see that all our neighbors need to hear good news.

## Four Kinds of Evangelism

1. $E_0$ refers to evangelism among nominal Christians to win these persons back to fervent faith.

In most of our churches there are inactive, complacent members. Their Christian attachment may be less important to them than their membership in a community club. And more may be required of them in the club than at church!

42

Your church can catch the vision of enfolding them back into a warm, caring fellowship, helping them to get involved again, encouraging them to grow. You will discover ways to teach them, to develop their concern for "growing in grace" and for social justice. Your nurture will motivate them to witness to their friends, some of whom are also in need of $E_0$ evangelism.

2. $E_1$ refers to the evangelism of non-Christians in one's own language and culture.

These people do not belong to any church and do not consider themselves Christians. In many cases they have rejected Christianity as out-of-date. They may have the belief that humanity is the center of the universe, and that if one tries hard enough and gains enough education and has enough money, there is need of little more.

Some have closer leanings to religious faith, but have not yet gotten the vision to send for "Peter." And "Peter" often stays in Joppa praying, taking no initiative to find them.

These are people who live all around your church. While you are praying, they may be knocking at your door. But we may be so loud in prayer that we cannot hear them in their need. For your church to grow, you may need to drop what you are doing—even if worthwhile—and walk with them, leading them step by step closer to God. For Peter, it took some time—days, in fact. It will also take time to reach people in your community.

3. $E_2$ refers to the evangelism of non-Christians who are separated from Christians because of a small but distinct cultural barrier.

Because these persons often have a different set of cultural values and may speak a different language, new churches may be formed just for these groups. It is generally difficult to assimilate them into existing churches.

Cornelius, his household, and many others in the Roman city of Caesarea (named for the Roman Emperor,

43

Caesar Augustus himself) could not have fit smoothly into the Jewish synagogue and culture. But through $E_2$ evangelism, they became Christians and worshiped and served the Lord in their context.

Your church may be challenged to begin a witness among those of a different ethnic background. The work will grow best if indigenous leadership can surface from among them. As the new church grows, they will relate to the home church and the home church to them on the basis of mutual support and love. The home church should not try to dictate policies or structures. These should be allowed to grow within the congregation, reflecting their own culture.

4. **$E_3$** refers to the evangelism of people whose culture and language are profoundly different from our own.

There are 2.4 billion or more non-Christians (Hindus, Buddhists, Marxists, Muslims, Animists) who have yet to believe in Jesus Christ. Most have yet to hear his name and what it really means. Your church may be in a denomination with a missionary agency which has developed the special skills needed to build this bridge. Missionaries need to learn another language, eat other food, and thoroughly adapt to another culture in another land if those persons will be reached.

Local congregations also send out mission workers from their churches. They pray and give to $E_3$ work. In our day some of these people also have been knocking on our front doors. They are the thousands of refugees who are being transplanted from countries in turmoil to ours. They are international students who are guests with us for several years. Will we come down off the rooftop to answer these knocks on our door?

Until Peter went to Caesarea, the Jewish believers carried on only an $E_0$ and $E_1$ mission. Now in the centurion's house, Peter launched the early church into an $E_2$ outreach. Before many years had passed Paul would take the mission a step further—to $E_3$ evangelism.

## Decision

We have the challenge for world evangelization to-day. Overwhelming? Thousands of Christians are answering the knock on their door, as Peter did. Will you join the team?

When the angel came to Centurion Cornelius, why did God ask the angel to tell Cornelius about Peter as the one who would bring him the message? So long as the angel was taking the time and effort to speak, why didn't he give the message of Jesus Christ himself? God could have spoken through the angel, but he wanted the gospel to be shared by Peter.

God is still seeking men and women to share the good news. He requires that we see no one as unclean or unacceptable. The good news is for all.

Your congregation can bridge the gap between Joppa and Caesarea. It can happen today!

# 7

# Prayer and Church Growth

*Acts 12:1-19*

## Getting Started

When I was three years old we moved to the country. My memories of that early age are sketchy, but I do recall vividly that we had a hand pump on our long front porch. When we wanted a drink, we had no faucet to turn. Instead, we would quench our thirst from the underground well.

If you've lived in similar circumstances, you know that when a pump is used frequently the water pours out with the first strike of the handle. But if it has not been used with regularity, the water level subsides, and the old screechy handle has to be worked up and down many times before getting any results.

The same is true with prayer. If you are keeping your pipe of communication open to heaven, your words will flow spontaneously from your heart whenever you wish to talk with God. But if you neglect to commune with him regularly, it becomes increasingly difficult to feel that someone is actually listening and responding. It is only through an open pipeline of prayer to God within our churches that they can be continually growing.

## Behind Closed Doors in Prayer

The book of Acts is a chain with each link a prayer

47

event. The early disciples bathed each other in prayer. Words denoting the use of prayer occur 35 times throughout Acts. Acts portrays a movement energized by prayer. And the church grew.

The church in this chapter of its life confronted prison bars with renewed freedom in prayer. James, the brother of John, was put to death. Now Peter was in jail, waiting for Herod's death knell.

But the Christians met together in prayer. "Peter could not be executed," they reasoned. Time was of essence. So they spent it praying. Note the seven essentials that gave prayer such prominence among them.

### 1. *Motivation for prayer* (v. 17)

According to Acts, early Christians did not have to be prodded, cajoled, prevailed upon, urged, or even encouraged to pray. They possessed a deep motivation that pressed them into prayer action.

When Peter returned to them after being miraculously delivered from prison, he had to motion for them to be quiet. This shows that a large roomful of people had gathered so that his voice could not be heard over the cacaphony of noise. Could this have been the "noise" of prayer?

The meeting did not consist of "two or three people gathered together," as in many prayer meetings today. A room full of prayer warriors gathered to face the foe. They cared about hurting people. Their motive for gathering to pray was not to fulfill an obligation to the church. Instead, it stemmed from hearts of love—love for their own and concern for the lost.

### 2. *Unity in prayer* (v. 5)

Was only one home cell group praying for Peter? With the rapid growth of the church, by Acts 4:4 there may have been a total of 8,000 to 11,000 disciples in Jerusalem. It would seem that not one, but many groups were interceding for Peter. Acts 5:12 says, "The church was earnestly praying." The people that night—alone or in groups, on moonlit housetops or in candlelit rooms—were unified in their prayers for Peter. It was only Mary's home cell group that was fortunate enough to see the immediate answer to their prayer.

The "church" in Acts 12:5 was following the example of the "all" in Acts 1:14. Here was total congregational praying—120 members—each a strong intercessor. A literal rendering is that they "persisted obstinately" in prayer.

### 3. *Spontaneity in prayer* (v. 12)

Because of the urgent need, many people no doubt left their homes and changed their plans in order to gather in prayer. News of Peter's arrest spread rapidly throughout the city. It was not long until a decision was made to pray together for Peter. The many groups that met together that night probably had not preplanned their meetings. It was not a regular time for gathering.

### 4. *Earnestness in prayer* (v. 5)

The King James Version uses the words "without ceasing." The New International Version has "earnestly." The original word, used only one other place in the New Testament (1 Pet. 4:8) means intensely, steadily, constantly. "Love each other *deeply*" (1 Pet. 4:8). This could have been Peter's last night alive. There was an intensity and earnestness which was probably unparalled in the history of the church.

### 5. *Focus in prayer* (v. 5)

The church was praying for Peter. It is clear that Peter was number one on their prayer list. Though they may have remembered the widow of James, and though they may have prayed for a steadfast faith for themselves, the focus was Peter. They did not pray around the world and back. They did not pray general, nebulous prayers. They were specific and their prayer request was clear.

### 6. *Faith in prayer* (vv. 12-15)

Although other essentials in prayer can be attributed to the small group of pray-ers in Mary's home cell group, faith seemed to be eluding them. Possibly it was the strong faith of the other hundreds or thousands of people that brought an answer to their prayer. This is not easily discernible.

But God did open the prison gates, and he did miraculously deliver Peter. Peter came back to the house of Mary and stood knocking at the door. One would think that Peter would have wanted cover as soon as possible. While Peter stood impatiently, waiting for Rhoda's return, the earnest pray-ers inside discussed the servant girl's trustworthiness and angelogy!

God certainly does at times answer a wavering faith, showing by his grace that he is still alive!

### 7. *Follow-up after prayer* (v. 17)

Peter insisted that others should be told about the answered prayer. "Tell James and the brothers about this." He knew that such a distinct answer to prayer would give them continued strength to go on. He knew that it would be a medium for developing congregational faith.

They did not neglect proclaiming the wonderful acts of God in answer to their prayer. Thus, prayer and proclamation formed the foundation upon which the early church was built. They proclaimed that Jesus was still alive and that he was in the process of building an ever-expanding community of faith.

## Prayer Power Needed Today

Why are many churches not growing and alive? Because prayer, the most central mark of religion, has been all but forgotten. Note all the religious elements mirrored in prayer—humility, trust, a sense of dependency, penitence, adoration, desire to be like God, triumph over sin, and a desire for eternal life. These are the characteristics we wish to develop in those yet to be won to Christ. Therefore we must ourselves be immersed in these characteristics, best conceived in prayer.

The great revivals of the past were prompted by prayer. In both Britain and the United States in the eighteenth and nineteenth centuries, persons gathered in groups to pray. The result? Great Wesley, Whitefield, Finney, Moody, Sunday, and Graham revivals exploded with excitement and religious fervor.

These seven essentials gave prayer special prominence in the early church. Where do you sense your church lacking? Look at them briefly, one by one. How can you best apply them to your local church?

### 1. *Motivation for prayer*

Motivation for prayer reflects the "temperature" of the church. Prayer meetings which are dull and dry are bereft of motivation. A living, growing church is a praying church. It is a church that believes in and practices the highest form of worship—prayer. A growing church is one that is motivated to pray for the unchurched, the needy, and the lost.

### 2. *Unity in prayer*

Today the church is thrust into the midst of a decadent society. When Christ built the church in the immoral and unjust Roman Empire, he first built a prayer meeting. How can we hope to see a revival in our churches when our prayer meetings are so weak? How can we expect to impact our communities for Christ when only a few people remember to pray for them? United prayer in the early church was the supreme method for accomplishing anything.

### 3. *Spontaneity in prayer*

A church today that is in the forefront of evangelism will plan ahead carefully and prayerfully. However, a church impassioned for the lives of sinners will not relegate all prayer time to a "Wednesday evening prayer meeting." It may be that a committee session is "interrupted" with a group prayer pertaining to a person or an issue at hand. It may be that after the benediction a group of persons chatting in the aisles will form a circle, and with hands clasped in unity, intercede for a special need.

### 4. *Earnestness in prayer*

Earnestness in prayer seems to be lacking among people today. A survey showed that lay people average four minutes per day and pastors seven minutes per day praying. When you gather for prayers how earnest or fervent are your prayers? How can your prayer times be elevated to the imperative and crucial? When you get a vision of the lostness of humanity and your own dependence upon God, your passivity will turn into urgency.

### 5. *Focus in prayer*

One writer said that prayer is better understood as a "focusing" of spiritual power rather than a verbalizing of requests to the Almighty. By praying in a conversational manner, the emphasis is not put on the one praying, but on the need being prayed about.

Prayer lists are helpful in focusing upon needs. Prayer for another in the prayer circle conveys affirmation and encourages spiritual strength. Specific answers to specific prayers can lead to specific praise to God. General prayers are quickly forgotten.

### 6. *Faith in prayer*

"Prayer is either a powerful force or a pitiful farce," said one minister. We may approach prayer so intellectually that we go through the motions without faith.

We can implant faith in the hearts of fellow Christians if we promise to back them up with our prayers, especially if they are undergoing stress. In some circles people stumble over the words, "I'll be praying for you." They promise only to be "thinking about one another." Yet we need more than each other's thoughts; we need their prayers.

A church that prays with faith is a church that believes in great possibilities. Why? Because they believe that God does hear and that he will act. But most of all, it is his will we seek, not the specific answer we wish would come.

### 7. Follow-up after prayer

We tend to see our prayer meetings as events that have a termination point. But these are only the beginnings. When you pray, expect something positive to result. Do not just pray without doing anything. When you pray alone or in a group, do something positive and concrete that the Lord can use. Use the prayer meeting as an inspiration for outreach.

## Decision

Prayer is God's opportunity. In prayer we give God the right to do what he's been wanting to do for a long time. God has provided salvation and the Holy Spirit. Now prayer fulfills the remaining essential condition to bring his covenant of grace into action. If we neglect prayer, we are failing God, and are making his plan of grace inoperable in our lives and in the souls of the lost.

If you want your church to grow, prayer must be a prominent practice and ministry among you. Allow Acts to happen among you today!

# 8

# Preparation for Mission

*Acts 11:19-30; 13:1-3*

## Getting Started

A revolutionary change had bolted the Jewish followers of Jesus into a new direction. When Cornelius was converted in Acts 10 the early followers of Jesus exclaimed, "So then, God has even granted the Gentiles repentance unto life" (Acts 11:18).

Changes in *thinking* are not always immediately translated into changes in *action*. In this case, months passed and then years before the meaning of Cornelius' conversion began to affect the evangelistic strategy of the young and growing church.

The change of a Palestinian Jewish religion to a religion that would embrace every nation of the world, calling all people to faith in Jesus, is the story of mission. That story has its beginning in Antioch.

## Mission Transmission from Antioch

Here in Antioch, in this large and cosmopolitan urban center, the first truly multicultural church was founded. Because Greek was the language of the city, rather than the Aramaic and Hebrew of Palestine, the followers of Jesus were given a new, Greek name. The Greek name for "Messiah" is "Christ," so the believers were first called Christians in Antioch (Acts 11:26).

Antioch, the capital of the Roman province of Syria, was the third largest city of the empire, next to Rome and Alexandria. It boasted of its magnificent temples and other public buildings erected by the Romans after their conquest of the city in 64 B.C. But though Antioch's appearance was impressive, its moral tone was degraded by orgiastic religious rites.

There certainly was a need for a transmission of the gospel in this decadent city. As this passage explains so well, Christianity did go forth. In fact, by the end of the fourth century, amidst a city population of 250,000, historians have estimated that Antioch may have contained as many as 100,000 Christians. During the period of A.D. 252-380 no less than ten church conferences were held there. It became known as the "mother church of Gentile Christianity."

What brought this Antiochan church into such prominence? Why did it become such a center for early Christianity?

1. *Gentiles were accepted as equal to Jews.*

The Jewish disciples at first preached only to fellow Jews. A change, however, was initiated by some Jews from Cyprus and Cyrene who "went to Antioch and began to speak to Greeks also ..." (Acts 11:20). As they converted persons to Jesus, they did not require an observance of the Jewish law. This slight change represents a remarkable growth in the understanding of God's mission to bring Jews and Gentiles together in the new community of Jesus.

This revelation would later be described by the mature missionary, Paul, as a mystery: "Through the gospel the Gentiles are heirs together with Israel, members together of one body, and sharers together in the promise in Christ Jesus" (Eph. 3:6). In Antioch the reality of this mystery, this miracle, was being lived out for the first time in the history of redemption.

## 2. The believers formed a relief agency.

A prophet, Agabus, predicted that a famine would spread over the entire Roman Empire. Such a famine did take place in Judea about A.D. 46.

This prophecy encouraged the Christians in Antioch to send a collection of money to help their brothers and sisters in Judea to buy food in preparation for the coming crisis. This act of Christian fellowship given voluntarily was an exciting development in mission. They reached outside their own community, sharing with persons they did not know because of a Jesus whom they were beginning to love. We see here an example of a "mother church" being helped by the "daughter church."

Their commitment to mission transmitted spiritual words into sacrificial giving. They entrusted Paul and Barnabas, their teachers and leaders, to take these famine relief funds on the 300-mile journey south to Jerusalem. A world vision was beginning to grow.

## 3. Antioch became a base for foreign missions.

After the threat of persecution, Acts describes the followers of Jesus haphazardly wandering from village to village preaching the good news. As a result of this dispersion, the seed of the gospel was planted in many locations. This was certainly a valid form of missionary activity—one that caused significant church growth.

Acts 13, however, tells about the beginning of a planned overseas mission carried out by representatives of a particular church. The missionaries were chosen by a deliberate church decision inspired by the Holy Spirit. Paul and Barnabas, the Antioch church's teachers, were being shared with the thousands of people yet engulfed in paganism.

The words of Ananias at Paul's conversion were becoming true. "This man is my chosen instrument to carry my name before the Gentiles and their kings and before the people of Israel" (Acts 9:15). The prophecy of Ananias was being fulfilled in a ministry far beyond the city limits of Antioch.

The first foreign mission had begun!

## Foreign-Mission-Oriented Congregations Today

What are the steps of preparation your congregation would have to take in order for it to become a modern-day Antioch? What will it take for your congregation to have a vision for the world? As you go over the following steps, based on the Acts account, check the areas in which you are strong, "so-so," and weak.

1. *Local evangelism* (Acts 11:20-21, 24)

Genuine involvement in mission begins with a burden for the lost in your own neighborhood. The church at Antioch saw new life springing forth among their neighbors in the city. As these new Christians were discipled and became acquainted with the heartbeat of God for a lost world, their vision was sharpened for those in need in other lands.

Our media exposure to world need has formed a crust of apathy over us. Even statistics indicating that millions have no knowledge of Jesus do not shake Christians out of lethargy. But local evangelism will sharpen our vision.

2. *Leadership* (Acts 11:22-26; 13:1)

Local evangelism and foreign mission both require good leadership. The church at Antioch was willing to accept two pastoral leaders from outside their fellowship so that they could be nurtured in the faith and equipped for ministry and mission. Three other leaders are mentioned in Acts 13:1 who were teachers and prophets.

Leaders who carry the "great commission" close to their heart and who challenge their congregations with the call of Christ to follow the home-to-world progression of Acts 1:8 will eventually see reluctance and apathy turn into compassion and commitment. As people are gently nurtured in church growth and missions concepts, many will eventually respond, though for some it may take a long time.

### 3. *Financial commitment* (Acts 11:27-30)

The Christians in Antioch learned stewardship of their wealth through the needs of the Jerusalem church. They were willing to give generously for the physical needs of others. This prepared them for their financial participation in an evangelistic mission to people even further away.

### 4. *Worship* (Acts 13:2)

Mission flows from worship in the community setting. Without a vision of God, we cannot have a proper understanding of the world. It was in the gathered congregation's worship that they heard the voice of the Spirit telling them to send out missionaries.

### 5. *Assigning responsibility* (Acts 13:2)

That which is everyone's work is no one's work! When the Lord gave the young church at Antioch a vision of the needs in Asia, they also were told to assign responsibility for doing the work. Mission requires the *setting apart* of persons for the many tasks that make possible the sharing of good news with peoples near and far away. The Antioch congregation sent out its most mature and able leaders!

### 6. *Fasting and prayer* (Acts 13:3)

The sending forth of the first two foreign missionaries was an act of faith. Faith can always be measured by prayer. Little prayer reflects little faith. Much prayer reflects great faith. Fasting, a discipline that most congregations have never known, has often been an evidence of the Spirit's work in renewal for mission.

## Decision

The world of 4.7 billion people has become our neighborhood. Three billion of these are not Christians. But *large numbers* do not seem to affect or phase many Christians today. Even when we break down these figures (e.g., 950,000,000 in China, 2,300,000 in Libya), the numbers are still incomprehensible. We cannot even imagine the faces of three billion lost people, much less imagine all that combined suffering.

We can be grateful that today many of our Christian brothers and sisters in other lands are themselves being sent out in mission. We can partner with them in the great task before us. But the challenge is to first reach those whose faces you already know—your kind aunt Millie, your cousin George, and the next-door neighbor. When you begin to reach those, and they reach other people whom they know, and they reach yet others, a web can be formed that will reach on and on around the globe.

The decision to begin that process is up to you. It can happen today!

# 9

# Church Planting

*Acts 14:21-28*

## Getting Started

Church planting is the formation of a new fellowship of believers. It is calling into being through the power of the Spirit, a new expression of Christ's body. Church planting is the birthing of a new family of faith.

The phrase, *Church planting* is not used in the New Testament, although Paul does speak at one point about "the one who *plants* and the one who *waters*" (1 Cor. 3:5-9). Paul is distinguishing here between gifts for *beginning* a new fellowship and gifts for *nurturing* it after it is started. The passage in this lesson gives us the first detailed account of a church planting mission in the New Testament.

## Asia Minor—A Major Church Planting Opportunity

Paul and Barnabas were selected by the believers in Antioch of Syria to move westward for the spreading of the gospel. They doubtless went to Cyprus first because it was the home of Barnabas, and then northward to Asia Minor, in regions just west of where Paul had lived and worked. The civilized, Roman world was their goal.

The universal use of the Greek language in Roman provinces was evidently a providential preparation for their mission. Another contribution to evangelization was that Judaism was espoused by pockets of people in many major towns and cities. This served as a bridge from paganism to Christianity.

If persons were to be enfolded within the care and love of God, new churches needed to be planted. Since Christianity had not spread westward with any significance, there were no churches for these new believers. Therefore Paul and Barnabas' aim was to begin in the chief cities of each district, since these were centers of influence.

These church planters then established within each city an organized church, one that soon developed beyond the "mission station" stage. As we shall see, each congregation was challenged by these church planters to take seriously spiritual growth and to make their church a center of witness to its community. That is certainly what happened. These churches were only the beginning of lively church plantings all across the Roman Empire and beyond.

Let us note, then, seven elements of church planting, based on the experience of Paul and Barnabas. Unless these ingredients are present, a strong, healthy, self-sustaining, and growing church cannot be established. Within these few verses of Acts 14:21-28 we see a picture of what church planting is all about.

### 1. Preaching the good news (v. 21)

Paul's visit with the people of Antioch of Pisidia (Acts 13:16-41) provides our first exposure to his thought and method as a preacher. As a beginning church planter, Paul knew that if he was to be effective, he would need to adapt his message to various audiences, even though he always began at the synagogue. Paul started with those who feared God, people who wanted to know God's intention for their lives. Paul began with what people knew, but he didn't stop there.

Paul's preaching brought people together to hear a

62

new word from God, a piece of good news. Jewish converts (Acts 13:43) and pagan Gentiles (Acts 13:48) both seemed ready to accept this word, but the preaching often provoked the wrath of the Jewish leaders. Paul began with Scriptures familiar to his hearers. Then carefully but forcefully, he introduced them to the life and teachings of Jesus. Jesus was always the center of Paul's sermons.

Preaching is important in church planting. The good news of Jesus must be publicly proclaimed. That proclamation is an important part of the foundation of a new congregation of believers. Fellowship is important, group Bible study helpful, and the development of mission vision essential. But the good news of Jesus must be publicly and vigorously proclaimed if the new church is to be firmly established as an expression, not just of a tradition, but of the new thing that God is doing in our world.

### 2. *Making disciples* (v. 21)

The clarity of the gospel message rang out amid the chaos of religious custom and pagan confusion. Those who were struck by the call and claims of this Jesus stepped out from Jewish tradition and heathenism to begin walking the road of discipleship. In Paul's scheme of building churches, initial belief was valid only when it became immersed in a new kind of lifestyle. Repentance was a change in both thinking and behavior.

The task of disciple-making is a time-consuming activity. As new persons are born into the Christian community, they must be discipled through Bible study, in one-to-one learning experiences, in small groups, and through personal spiritual disciplines.

Growth will also occur when love is modeled in action and when Christians are helped to discover, develop, and use their spiritual gifts. To make disciples is to bring persons into responsible membership into Christ's body. It is helping new believers "to grow up in Christ," to measure up to full stature (Eph. 4).

### 3. *Strengthening the fellowship of believers* (v. 22)

As Paul and Barnabas retraced their steps through Lystra, Iconium, and Antioch, they were concerned that people had truly been brought together in close-knit fellowships. These early church planters were well aware that a few new Christians in a hostile environment need close relationships. Christianity must be nourished in fellowship. New Christians cannot survive as isolated individuals.

"The Bible," said Samuel Johnson, "knows nothing of solitary religion." Church planting is an evangelism that brings individuals and families to Christ, restoring fellowship among persons and groups of persons. Church planting is a social ministry because Christ's life transforms both personal and societal relationships.

### 4. *Encouragement to authentic faith in the face of opposition* (v. 22)

These two master church planters had embarked on a mission that entailed persecution. They returned to Antioch of Syria by going through the very cities which persecuted them. They gave warning to the new believers, frankly telling them that they would be able to enter the kingdom of God only through affliction. Certainly when the going got tough, these converts from a pleasant paganism would be tempted to return.

Is American paganism much different from Roman paganism? As new believers join a newly planted church, expectations by family and close friends can lead to taunts of persecution. The walk of faith can be painful for the new Christian. The new congregation must be helped to understand the meaning of suffering and disappointment.

### 5. *Appointment of congregational leaders* (v. 23)

Paul and Barnabas, the church planters, were always quick to affirm the leadership gifts which the Spirit was bringing to the fledgling fellowship. The "elder" role was probably patterned after a Jerusalem model.

Identified leaders were to be true spiritual guides to their sisters and brothers in the newly found faith. They were looked to for encouragement and instruction in the face of the hardship and persecution they would inevitably face as they followed a Messiah who had died by capital punishment.

In a newly planted church today, the discovery, development, and use of the leadership gifts of local persons is imperative if the church is to be established and grow. This trust in local leadership is the foundation for authentic church growth, showing people that this church is "our church," not a "project" owned and operated by a district executive, a mother church, or a pastor from outside.

### 6. Training in prayer and fasting (v. 23)

Paul and Barnabas were sent on this important missionary journey after prayer and fasting (Acts 13:3), and they were intent on teaching these principles to the new Christians. It was with prayer and fasting that they commended these newly appointed elders to the Lord. These spiritual disciplines were also necessary for the church to grow.

When a new church is born, that new community is a reflection of God's life. That divine life is sustained by the Word of God, understood and applied through the spiritual disciplines of study, prayer, and fasting.

### 7. Reporting back to the sponsoring church (v. 27)

Paul and Barnabas carried the news of God's saving acts back to the church at Antioch, the congregation that had sent them forth on this first historic mission assignment. The Antioch church had a natural interest in the wonderful story their missionaries had to tell.

Church planting is always an apostolic activity,

involving the sending forth of messengers, and receiving back again those who have carried forth the good news. The successes of a new church can become milestones for the sending church, and it is strengthened all the more.

## Planting Churches Today

Why plant churches today? Aren't there enough churches already? Shouldn't we be nurturing existing ones rather than starting new ones? Don't new churches just confuse things, bringing a competitive spirit to the body of Christ?

There are four important reasons for church planting:

*1. Church planting fulfills the great commission.*

If we are to "make disciples" according to Matthew 28:19-20, then we must also provide a family for these newborn children of God. Sometimes there are existing fellowships to care for the new believers. But sometimes new churches must be formed to care for the new disciples. When we are obedient to the great commission, we will plant new churches.

*2. Church planting encourages reproduction.*

God has so arranged the human family that the young and inexperienced parents give birth to children. Parents who have many years of experience retire from the responsibility of birthing new family members.

The beginning of new families makes possible the birth of children and new combinations of personal and family traits. Without the planting of new homes, and the planning for new families, the human race would become extinct.

So it is with the church. The planting of a new fellowship leads naturally to spiritual reproduction, to new believers being born into the family of God. As churches grow older, they tend naturally to spin off new

66

and spiritually younger congregations.

Parent congregations are dignified by wisdom and strength; "planter churches" are enthusiastic with vision for evangelism and growth.

*3. Church planting allows new ministries to emerge in order to meet the changing needs of a community.*

New fellowships are able to diagnose and respond to the needs of a community more effectively than can existing congregations with established philosophies of ministry and program.

*4. Church planting is an effective response to cultural diversity.*

People are different, and no one congregation can meet the needs of all persons and cultures, especially in an urban community. New churches can focus on particular groups of persons in a community who are yet unreached by the good news of Jesus.

## Decision

Is your congregation planning to give birth sometime in the future? Congregational reproduction or church planting is not only for distant lands. It is a challenge for the church in every generation, region, and community.

# 10

# Unity and Growth

*Acts 15:1-35*

## Getting Started

Some people may feel that a growing church is a problem-free church. They think that discord and friction are dispelled in the face of new people and creative programming.

However, the opposite is many times true. The example in Acts 15 reflects this. The preaching to the Gentiles and the influx of non-Jews into the fellowship produced a serious problem that needed a solution without which the church could have dwindled to nothing.

## The Jerusalem Council: A Time for Discernment

The church leaders were committed to the great commission. Paul and Barnabas, as well as other disciples would not ignore any problem that could cause disunity and hinder evangelistic progress. They were willing to interrupt missionary journeys in order to clarify missionary policy. However, these policies would be tailored to the needs of a growing church. We see throughout the New Testament Epistles that Christian beliefs and practice were shaped by a concern for an ongoing mission. If the early church would not have been serious about growth and the inclusion of all people, we would have a very different New Testament today.

When controversy arose, how did these early Christian disciples respond?

1. *They discovered the problem* (vv. 1-5).

What was the problem that led to this special gathering of apostles and elders in Jerusalem? It was this: Gentiles were becoming Christians. So the question arose, "If a Gentile wants to be a follower of Jesus, must the new disciple become a Jew? Or could some of the Jewish regulations be ignored by new believers who did not share these religious traditions?" Some of the Christian Jews wanted them to be circumcised and to keep the law of Moses.

Early Jewish Christians insisted on circumcision for all believers, even if they were not born Jewish. If new Gentile Christians did not accept these Jewish traditions, they were therefore ritually unclean and were excluded from fellowship with strict Jewish Christians. The problem was most acute when the church met to "break bread."

Now through the efforts of Paul and Barnabas and other evangelists, the problem was coming out into the open. They were convinced that the Gentile mission was jeopardized by the strict requirements of the Palestinian leaders. Paul and his cohorts were preaching grace, and the "men ... from Judea" (v. 1) were preaching law. It was imperative that this conflict be resolved so that the Gentile churches could be united in faith with the Jewish congregations in Palestine. But the first step was to identify the problem. This was the first item on the Jerusalem Conference agenda.

2. *They discussed the issues* (vv. 6-12).

The apostles and elders knew that if a problem like this would remain unsolved, the thrust of the gospel would be impeded. So they did not stop with identifying the problem. They examined the issues carefully with the intention of finding a solution. The text indicates that there was sharp disagreement and rigorous discussion on the question.

The deliberations of those days in Jerusalem included all the apostles and elders present, not just Paul, Peter, and James. There was time for open discussion (v. 7) so that all could have a chance to contribute what they had to say. When there is conflict in the church, there must be the broadest possible participation in the airing of the issues. Both sides must be heard.

After a vigorous discussion, everyone listened to Peter's presentation of the historical background of the situation (vv. 7-11). The key question regarding the basis of salvation was answered clearly by Peter. He said that both Jews and Gentiles alike have to *believe* in order to be saved by the grace of God. But obedience to the Mosaic law would not be required of Gentiles.

Even the believing Pharisees, who had taken a very "Jewish" stand (v. 5), humbly listened to those who had been on the cutting edge of mission activity. This more parochial group must have been impressed with the way God was working in new and miraculous ways among the Gentiles, and they remained silent (v. 12).

3. *They discerned the solution* (vv. 13-21).

James, the recognized leader of the Jerusalem church, then spoke. He drew the discussion together, putting into words the emerging concensus of the young church. Though he had been a rigorous observer of the law and the crown of orthodoxy, James was able to identify with the Gentiles, giving a strong appeal to persons of both persuasions.

Acts 15 was a community discernment process. But James took leadership in bringing the debate to a focus and conclusion. He suggested a compromise that was both scripturally sound and culturally acceptable (v. 20).

Had the compromise been more strict, it would have choked the life out of evangelistic activity among the Gentiles. If it had been more tolerant, it might have alienated the Christian Jews. The principle was finally established that Jew and Gentile were one in Christ in fulfillment of the Scriptures.

4. *They dispatched the news* (vv. 22-35).

With the future of Gentile congregations at stake, the church leaders wasted no time telling the good news abroad. When the decision was reached, they described it carefully in a letter, probably with signatures of some or all who attended the Jerusalem Conference. This authoritative letter was not impersonally sent by public courier. It was entrusted to Judas and Silas who went along with Paul and Barnabas to Antioch (v. 22). There was a personal touch to the news. A letter alone could have sounded coldly official. But the warm words of the quartet who returned to Antioch bearing the letter, assisted in its acceptance by both the Jewish and Gentile Christians there.

In order to foster further unity among the Antiochan church, Judas and Silas, who were viewed as prophets (v. 32), remained with these Christians for a period of time encouraging and strengthening them. Along with other evangelists, Paul and Barnabas continued in responsible missionary activity with a new freedom and fervor, telling the good news to Jew and Gentile alike (v. 35).

## Today's "Growing Church" Council:
## Solutions that Aid Mission

The church that grows, continually adding persons of all walks of life, is a church that works through issues to find unity on matters of faith and practice. New people need to see unity, not discord, with respect to the disciplines of the Christian life. These "Gentiles," not reared in your congregational family or religious culture, realize that certain things must change in their lives as they transfer from American "paganism" to Christianity. Are these new expectations the voice of tradition alone or do they carry the authority of Jesus himself? It is the word of Christ that brings unity.

Is there controversy today in your church, even as at the Jerusalem Conference, over unsettled issues or unresolved conflicts? Are you facing issues over which there seems to be no clear "Thus saith the Lord"? In our churches we wrestle with worship patterns, issues of dress and outward appearance, divorce and remarriage, political involvement, among other things. How do we make decisions regarding these questions? Has your congregation found answers which allow the "Gentiles" who join you to see that the members are unified and working together in love? Do new members feel fully respected and included by your approach to questions of faith and culture? Or do they feel that they must give up the good of their own culture in order to put on a new "religious" culture?

If a church has settled *all* issues, it is probably either in need of a proper burial or is so heavenly that it needs a reincarnation! However, certain issues, if not dealt with properly, will soon choke the joy of Christian fellowship and the church's outreach will be stifled. If you have a church with issues like this, what can you do?

The Acts 15 model is helpful. Congregational decision-making can be stifled by anger and competition. The outcome will depend upon the attitudes displayed and the methods employed. Creative compromise that is true to Scripture is a spiritual gift, not a watering down of the gospel. It is often arrogance rather than concern for the truth that prevents the kind of Spirit-led compromise reached in the Jerusalem Conference.

Unity with its resulting growth comes to our churches only if we back up congregational decisions with tender expressions of love. Cold policy without warm presence is of little value. It may even work against church growth and success. But unity tempered with love will have a drawing power that will, as in the book of Acts, blaze the trail to continued growth.

I was personally present in two different meetings where a decision needed to be made. One meeting was interrupted with people bitterly stampeding out in disgust. The other meeting was punctuated with prayer. These took place in two different churches over essentially the same issue. The first resulted in further problems until the issue that could have helped the church grow was dropped altogether. In the second meeting, the issue was worked through in love and understanding.

Members must be unified if they wish their church to grow. Often we see a "spider mentality" in our churches. A spider decides on her own where and how to build her web. All by herself she anchors the web to withstand wind and weather. And when properly constructed it is an intricate web of rare beauty. But it is built by the spider for the spider to catch other unsuspecting insects for the spider's diet. The spider works by herself and for herself. Where is the cooperation among other spiders? Where is teamwork in facing a foe or catching the prey?

Maybe some of us are like this. Instead of demonstrating brotherhood through discussion and compromise, working together to create something much larger than any of us, we take pride in our own accomplishments, weaving our own web for our own satisfaction.

When we feel that the life of the church must revolve around our own particular convictions and desires, refusing to listen or to compromise, the church suffers. But the church in which Christians strive, plan, and pray for unity in attitude and action—that congregation will be effective in its ministry and its mission.

## Decision

A Spirit-led church is open to all. In Acts 10 Peter learned the truth that God is no respecter of persons. The church began to grow. Church growth is possible for you today only if your church is unified in a desire to open its doors to all. Accept people as they are. Love them and share with them the good news of Jesus, so that they can grow in faith. This is the unified and growing church. Are you ready to reach out in love to the "undesirables" in your neighborhood?

# 11

# Good News in the City

*Acts 17:22-34*

## Getting Started

Paul's ministry began in the city of Damascus and ended in the city of Rome. He was spurred on from city to city because of the great spiritual need he felt in these centers of civilization. The concentration of people presented a challenge to Paul and his colleagues. But why the city? Why Antioch, Ephesus, Thessalonica, Berea, and now Athens?

## The Athenian Atheists

These cities of the Roman Empire were diverse in every way—racially, spiritually, and intellectually. Athens, years before Paul's time, had gained prominence as a cultural center. Though the art, sculpture, and exquisite structures remained, the city now dominated the empire as a center of culture and philosophy and religion. Athens was the great university city of the Roman world.

Because this city was a center for learning, the air seemed alive with new ideas and philosophies. Scholars taught and discussed the varied secular and atheistic philosophies which stood in such bold contrast to Paul's God-centered message. Paul in his teaching described a God who created the universe and who cared so much about creatures of his world that he planned for their eternal salvation, not just temporary satisfaction. His explanation of the "Unknown God" ends with the good news of the resurrection (v. 31).

The two main philosophies that were in vogue among the scholars in that day were Epicureanism and Stoicism. The Epicureans taught that the chief aim of existence is pleasure—that pleasure is the only good, and pain is the only evil. For them the gods did not exist. Or, if they did, they were too far from the world to exercise any influence on what was happening. They were not really sensualistic, however. Instead, they had a lofty view of "pleasure" and scorned sensualism.

Stoicism, founded by Zeno (340-265 B.C.), took its name from the *stoa* or colonnade where he taught. Stoics believed that God was everything and in everything. If God is part of man, then there is no difference between the human and the divine. Man becomes his own god. Stoic ethics stressed individual self-sufficiency and obedience to the call of duty.

These philosophers began to dispute with Paul in the marketplace (vv. 17-18). But they were so intrigued with this new "philosophy" that they invited Paul to "a meeting of the Areopagus" (v. 19). This was likely an unofficial gathering of some Athenians on a hill near the Acropolis, overlooking the marketplace.

This occasion gave Paul an opportunity to spell out his views. Although Paul's position was directly opposed to the popular beliefs, he was able, through the Spirit of God, to build bridges of understanding with these sophisticated Greek philosophers (vv. 22-23). He chose to talk about one of their own gods, one that had no name, and whose altar bore the inscription "To the Unknown God." Paul went on to preach about this "Unknown God" declaring it to be the one true God. This God, said Paul, had revealed himself in showing his power and authenticity by raising Christ from the dead (vv. 24-31).

Paul's ministry in Athens yielded only a few

converts—people who believed in Jesus and the resurrection (v. 34). Two of these were Dionysius and Damaris. But who knows how many others were converted through their witness in the generations that followed? Tradition says that Dionysius became the first Bishop of Athens.

Though we are not sure about the results in Athens, we know that Paul was able to begin a number of churches in cities of the early Roman world. Christianity began to spread. Paul was forced to cross a number of barriers in the cities in which he preached. He and other witnessing Christians leaped over many social, cultural, and political walls in order to give birth to new churches. Persons of all backgrounds were welcomed into these fellowships.

## Today's City—a Target for the Gospel

The "Paul" who preaches to the "Athens" of today performs on the same stage as that of the first century. Many gods are worshiped in the secular city. Christians today must thread their way through these altars to find the place of the "Unknown God" for which our cultures still search. Today the gods are made of stocks and bonds, of culture and education, of the arts and sciences, of military might and national security, of pleasure and amusement. But something is amiss, and somewhere in the city are found those who seek for another god, an unknown god that is yet to be found.

If church growth is to take place in America and around the world in the years to come, the Christian church must recover a vision of the great cities of the world. Our population in North America is now 75 percent urban, and by the year 2000 it is expected that in North America nine out of ten people will live in the city.

Somewhere in the world a new London-sized city (a city with 10 million people) emerges every 45 days. By the year 2000 the world's 60 largest cities will contain 650 million people. It is quite clear that the cities must be at

79

the very center of our church growth and mission strategy.

Some Christians today would like to defend, insulate, and even isolate themselves and their families from the city, feeling that staying away will aid separation from the world. But if there is such a preponderance of evil in the city, who better can initiate change than Christians equipped with the whole armor of God? The city will change and the church will grow when Christians, like Paul, take up residence in the Athens and Corinths of the modern world. Dedicated followers of Jesus will take the city by befriending, loving, and caring for people, showing the resurrection power of the "Unknown God."

Let us look at some results of the good news in the city today.

1. *The gospel overcomes racism and social prejudice.*

Living in southern California among blacks, Anglos, Hispanics, and Orientals was a special blessing for me. I pastored a church in the inner city. Though traditionally white in membership, I watched it begin to take on a different complexion. It was exciting. But crossing those racial barriers was a struggle. Our cultural ties bound us to each other. Our common religious heritage tended to shelter us from close relationships with persons from different cultural backgrounds. Even deliberate strategy seemed to run aground.

Hard work and patience can bring success in reaching across ethnic, social, and intellectual barriers. Paul probably did not spend enough time in Athens to do that. He planted a few seeds and moved on. Others were left to water the seed and nurture the new plant. Antioch of Syria, Ephesus, Philippi, Corinth, and Rome, however, demonstrate Paul's commitment to a gospel that overcame race and class prejudice so that Jesus could be preached to all urban dwellers.

2. *The good news speaks to physical and social needs.*

The church in some parts of the city today is faced with deplorable conditions under which people barely eke out an existence. The church must minister to the whole person. But if we are to serve, we cannot serve with the attitude, "We are here to help. Here is how we'll do it." Rather we must go as servants—listening to them and responding to their needs.

We can learn from them and they from us. They can help us and we them. Christians have needs that are met only as we reach out in love—needs met only through interdependence.

3. *The good news builds friendships.*

Loneliness may be the number one disease of modern life. Census Bureau statistics show that the number of Americans living alone increased much faster than the general population during the 1970s. The number of households containing only one person rose 64 percent to 17.8 million between 1970 and 1980.

Friendship evangelism has in recent years become a part of our vocabulary. But how many Christians in our churches make deliberate efforts to search out persons in need of a friend? Much of the violence and crime in our cities could be curtailed if these offenders had sincere, loyal friends who truly cared. Much delinquency is a cry for attention, for someone to listen and care. Are we Christians ready to respond to those distorted cries for help? Or do we join others around us in building higher walls to separate us from them?

Friendship includes being a good listener. It means initiating activities that can be enjoyable for both. Friendships established by attending an athletic event with someone or by sharing a picnic in the city park can lead to a shared Bible study, and into the first steps of Christian faith.

4. *The good news broadens community.*

Without a Spirit-implanted love for the lost in the city, Christians will tend to stay among their own kind of people. However, those of other racial and cultural backgrounds will reach out their hands for acceptance and community when they see Christians demonstrating the openness of the community of faith.

Before we talk about Jesus, we may need to first learn another language, to eat a different food, to rebuild a house, to make a friend. But when we become friends we will not stop with these matters of home and culture. We care. Our new friend will want to understand what inspires us. In time this friend may become a friend of Jesus and a loyal member of our own congregation.

The church in the city must assimilate these new friends. Why evangelize if they are not welcome within the fellowship? How will they be surrounded with love and support? We must not allow cultural or racial prejudice to exclude those whom Christ has accepted. We must open our doors so that all may come in.

## Decision

Paul went from city to city planting churches and building the new community. He broke down walls and invited all people to enjoy the Christian way of life. If your church is in the country, will someone go to reach the city dweller? If your church is in the suburbs, are you discovering the hurts and cries of those caught in the webs of tangled family relationships, heartache, and depression? If your church has been placed in the inner city, will you continue to make special efforts to open doors of hope and compassion to those of your neighborhood? What can your church do to reach the city?

The young, the old, the rich, and the poor are all welcome. All can find peace and security, hope and friendship. Is your congregation ready to declare "The Unknown God?" It can happen today!

# 12

# Politics and the Kingdom

*Acts 25:6-12*

## Getting Started

God has called a people to live out his highest intentions in order to build a new community, the kingdom of God. However, these "called out" ones sometimes swerve away from his divine wishes and begin to carry on their own program. Note the group of Jews who brought charges against Paul. They wielded their own "political power" in order to destroy Paul's ministry, though evidences for their charges were unsubstantiated. But Paul, too, took advantage of his own political power—his Roman citizenship—as a way of taking his message to the very heart of the Roman Empire—to Rome itself.

Do these same kinds of politics take place in the local church today? Can "church politics" hinder evangelistic outreach? When should a Christian "appeal to Caesar?"

## Paul: Jewish Convict or Roman Citizen?

Paul was gripped by God's mission. Ever since the day of his conversion on the road to Damascus, he had been given over to preaching the good news of Jesus. The mission of his entire life had become its message. "Woe to me if I do not preach the gospel!" was the heartfelt sentiment that Paul exclaimed to the Corinthians (1 Cor. 9:16).

Paul's particular mission, which dates to the time of his baptism, was to take the gospel to the Gentiles (Acts 9:15). Paul was so gripped by this divine mandate that even when he was under arrest, he continued to react as a missionary. Not only was he imprisoned for his faith, Paul was ready at every moment to use his imprisonment as an occasion for witness.

Note Paul's response in our background text. Paul had been a prisoner for the sake of Christ in Caesarea. Festus, the new procurator, had just returned to Caesarea from a short visit to Jerusalem, bringing with him a deputation from the Sanhedrin. Paul was brought to court where his accusers were given opportunity to bring charges. These indictments could not be substantiated, however. Paul denied them all, declaring that he had done nothing against Jewish law or against the sanctity of the temple.

Although Festus as the newly appointed governor of Judea wished to earn the good graces of this influential Jewish group, he could find nothing to convict Paul. Perhaps if Paul went back to Jerusalem for a third trial there would be more convicting grist for the governor's mill. After all, a larger contingent of Paul's Jewish enemies resided there. No doubt he knew that in Jerusalem Roman justice might be overrun by powerful local influences.

Another alternative available to Roman citizens was appeal to the Caesar in Rome. Paul knew that by standing trial before Caesar, he could avoid unfair Jewish "politics." But another thought may have flashed in his missionary mind. If this appeal would be granted, he would be provided a free trip to Rome. He could carry the name of Jesus to Rome itself. There he could appear before the very power structure that shaped policy, practice, and belief for the entire Western world. Though not a young man anymore, Paul was less concerned about his safety than he was with the progress of the gospel.

Paul was one of the privileged few to hold Roman citizenship, even though he came from one of Rome's conquered provinces. While Paul did not flaunt his privileged status, neither did he ignore it. Here was a chance to "use the system" to gain a toehold for the gospel.

Political involvement, or use of his political rights, was never for Paul an end in itself. The goal was always to make disciples for Jesus. Every decision, every political alternative was weighed in the light of that unvarying priority.

## Church Politics: For Which Kingdom?

What does all of this have to say about today's local congregation that wishes to grow? When there is a stirring of the Spirit, when new people are being folded into the church, and when program shifts appear which help to assimilate them, a reaction generally occurs. This negative sentiment most easily arises within churches that have not grown in numbers for many years.

If this is happening in your church, you may attempt to separate in your mind the elements which truly reflect the kingdom of God and those which come from human tradition. What are the unchanging rules? What is human tradition? When a church grows, the new people may find no meaning in some of the traditions which have accumulated over the years. What can one do?

Festus, being a newly appointed governor, wanted to gain the good will of these Jews without infringing on Roman justice. A newly appointed pastor who believes deeply in church growth, in reaching out to the spiritual needs of the community, also desires to build rapport with church leadership. But what if the leaders are more interested in maintenance than growth? What if they feel threatened by new members who prove themselves as strong leaders?

"Church politics" in its good sense is the proper management of authority and lines of communication so that God is honored and people are built up. Good management and organization are needed so that leaders and members work together for the good of all.

"Church politics" in its negative aspect, however, happens when persons use power selfishly for their own ends. The temptation comes to pastor and people alike to take the easy way out by becoming popular with those who may either formally or informally hold the power. Festus attempted to play up to the strict Jews in order to build a more solid power base in Judea. Festus was "saved" from his selfishness by Paul's appeal to Caesar.

From another point of view, Paul was being held in detention because of "church politics." It was a conflict among God's people about church standards that had gotten Paul in trouble in Jerusalem. Strict Jewish believers were convinced that Paul was compromising the truth of God's Word in his evangelistic ministry to the Gentiles.

Paul, however, was unwilling to remain paralyzed by church politics. He did not wish to return to Jerusalem where the religious issues would continue to be debated for years while others in the Roman world further west waited to hear the good news of Jesus.

Paul used a secular political process—the appeal to Caesar—to escape church politics. Paul used his Roman citizenship to prevent the paralysis of God's mission by an endless religious debate. Such debate may have proven who in the end was more forceful and convincing. But it would motivate no one to extend the kingdom of God. Paul went on to evangelize as far as Rome (and perhaps even in Spain) while the theologians in Jerusalem continued in their debates about church standards.

What is the main purpose of your church? To be spiritually pure? To maintain the status quo? To nurture all present believers? To make sure biological growth takes place? To enjoy comfortable worship services?

These are not unworthy goals. The main purpose of the church, however, should be to advance the gospel. This does not come about by clever persuasion, religious debate, or political force. Constantine in the fourth century naively baptized his armies in the river, sending them forth to battle. The Crusades in the medieval period commissioned men, women, and children in a tragic fight to regain the "Holy Land." But the Christian church today conquers by love.

## Decision

As you make a definite decision now to be more aggressive in mission outreach, give serious attention to the conflicts which keep your congregation from reaching out. How does your church relate to newcomers? Do these newcomers find their way into leadership positions? What issues might require members of your congregation to "appeal to Caesar"? Are you willing, with Paul, to use a political right or process when necessary to further the progress of the gospel? Are you able as a fellowship to turn your back on religious controversy so that you may take the good news of Jesus to others? Determine now that politics, within the congregation or without, shall be placed at the service of the gospel.

# 13

## Growth Through Restriction

*Acts 28:16-31*

### Getting Started

Problems which arise in the life of our churches can be overcome by our greater reliance on God. When "restrictions" occur in the ebb and flow of our congregational witness, we cannot be passive or self-sufficient in our outreach. But we are not really restricted when the Holy Spirit recreates our thinking!

### Paul Chained in Prison

Paul's appeal to Caesar brought him finally to Rome. He was allowed to live in his own house under the guard of a soldier. No more could he come and go as he pleased. Had he been free, he might have visited several synagogues located in this imperial city. But instead of lamenting this restriction, he invited the leaders of the Jewish community to come to him.

Paul's physical imprisonment did not hinder his opportunity. As he faced the Jewish leaders, Paul did not make a complaint against the Jewish nation or the leaders in Judea. Instead he shared his devotion to the ancestral hope of Israel. He emphasized that the Christian message which he had preached from city to city was God's fulfillment of the religion of Israel (vv. 17-21).

The Jewish authorities became interested. They

brought more people along to hear this message. Paul spent a full day explaining to them the content. of the Christian faith, trying to convince them about Jesus from their own Scriptures. Some were convinced, but many turned away (vv. 23-24).

Paul, sensing a replay of what happened so many times before in his ministry (some convinced, others skeptical), proceeded to quote Isaiah 6:9-10 in which Isaiah was warned not to expect a favorable response from the people. But restriction and rejection issued into hope as Paul prophesied that the Gentiles would respond favorably to this new message (vv. 25-28).

Although restricted, Paul's witness continued. Though he was kept in custody for two more years, anyone could come and visit him. Paul was no longer in the hinterlands of Pisidia or Asia Minor. He was in the capital city of Rome, the heart of the empire! To this crossroads of civilization peoples of all races and backgrounds came.

The growth of the Christian church would be inspired for years because of Paul's restriction, though not even Paul knew it at the time. It was here in prison that Paul wrote Philippians, Ephesians, Colossians, and Philemon. Other missionaries and church planters like Luke, Aristarchus, Timothy, and Mark would be inspired for all time by his "church growth seminars."

The soldiers who guarded Paul were members of the select troops of the emperor, the Praetorian Guard. Paul's being chained to the emperor's men was no restriction at all so far as Paul's life purpose was concerned. Even hardened soldiers can soften up to the gospel when it is heard from the lips of a compassionate Paul. And what an ideal channel to the emperor himself!

## Overcoming Restrictions Today

What restrictions to church growth do you face at this time in your congregational life? As you reflect on these seven common growth-restricting obstacles, ask what you can do to overcome them and discover new horizons of outreach waiting for your church.

1. *"Our church is too small."*

Sometimes this excuse is given for not trying to reach out and receive new people in your church. Concerned members in the small church say, "We don't have enough children for a well-graded Sunday school program. Our few youth go to other youth fellowships because we are not large enough to provide for them at church. Our budget is so low we cannot provide full support for a pastor."

Most large churches began on a small scale. Patient, deliberate prayer, witness, and programming will begin to build momentum. Offer what people in your community need. Small churches have some advantages, too. But if it is to be faithful, it must be evangelistic.

2. *"Our church is too large."*

Perhaps you feel that your church is too large already. Persons who for years have been in a growing church may wake up one day and realize that they do not know everyone's first name. "It's not like it used to be when we were all like one big happy family," they say. "It's just not the same."

The family idea is important, but instead of barring the doors to new persons, think of creative ways to maintain a close fellowship. Remember that one's personal desire to "keep tabs" on each church member is much less important than sharing a loving home for all who wish to come.

At what point does any church member have the audacity to say to a newcomer, "We're sorry, we're large enough. You will have to try to find another church." What if the cutoff would have come just before you decided to come?

### 3. *"Our church is a retirement center."*

"Most of our people are older," you may say. "How will we ever grow?" Within one church I pastored one sixth of the people were 80 years old or more. We were surrounded by a number of senior citizens' homes. Over a short period of time we were able to include four new members over 70. One of these had become a new child of God after being away from the Lord for many years.

You probably have in your community seniors who are unchurched and lonely. Many older people have time to minister effectively to persons their own age. Capitalize on this gift. Reach out with this age as your target. I have noticed that older people sometimes welcome innovations more than others. They could be an encouragement to growth even among the younger.

### 4. *"Our church is a drive-in church."*

"We have a commuter church," you might say. "People drive in from 20 miles away and very few live in our immediate neighborhood. We can't grow very well because we can't expect neighbors of these commuters to drive that far to church." That could indeed be a hindrance to growth.

But this also holds advantages. Hundreds of people live between your church and its distant members—hundreds that can be reached for Christ.

However, if you wish to develop more of a community church atmosphere, build with the members who are near the church. Reach their webs of relationships. Develop ministries that will meet the needs of those persons. Make sure the community knows that your church cares about them.

### 5. *"Our church is an exclusive club."*

"Our present members don't reach out to newcomers when they do come," you might say. Yes, many churches are very much ingrown. Visitors are not recognized very well. Conversations that take place after church are among people who have been friends for years.

How can this restriction be overcome? Church leaders and pastors can model friendship. Deliberately pair off present members with new people in a friendship partnership plan. Set up a hospitality committee in your church that will work diligently at splitting apart this very serious restriction to church growth.

### 6. "Our church is too different."

"We have beliefs in our denomination that are unique and probably will not be acceptable to some," is another anti-growth excuse. It is true that all denominational groups have their unique beliefs. That is why denominations have arisen. But millions of people are unchurched, and many would go if they had a welcome.

They may respond to your love and eventually grow into espousing your beliefs. They will be wooed to your church first when they see this caring and love from your people. A "peculiar" doctrine becomes more palatable when a newcomer is accepted and loved. Accept the person, and he or she may accept the doctrine.

We must also remember that some people are looking specifically for what your church has to offer and what it believes.

### 7. "Our church is surrounded by problems."

"We are in the midst of a declining neighborhood," you may say. "Our neighborhood is very poor. It's a mixture of races and cultures. There are a lot of social problems and crime."

That is precisely where the church is needed. Churches in these areas must generate ministries that will bring healing—ministries that will turn upside down negative psychological structures. Train your people in how to work with, counsel, witness to, and accept all people, regardless of race or background.

## Decision

Paul overcame restrictions by creatively taking advantage of every opportunity. We can positively face these obstacles today.

God asks us in our churches to not be overcome with evil—that is, be overwhelmed by supposed restrictions we perceive—but to overcome evil with good. Though we cannot remove all growth-restricting obstacles, we will be able with God's help to remove a few and be faithful and successful in our mission and ministry. "When I am weak," Paul wrote, "then I am strong!"

Through God's power, it can happen today!

# Coauthor

G. Edwin Bontrager is pastor of the Neffsville Mennonite Church near Lancaster, Pennsylvania. He has also served for five years as chairperson of the Evangelism Commission of the Atlantic Coast Conference of the Mennonite Church.

A native of Williamsville, New York, he received his Doctor of Ministry degree from Fuller Theological Seminary, Pasadena, California, in 1976. He received his B.D. degree from Eastern Mennonite Seminary in 1966 and his B.A. degree from Eastern Mennonite College in 1963.

Following his graduation from EMC, he served the college as admissions counselor. Moving to northern Ohio, he became Bible instructor at Central Christian High School in Kidron and served as pastor at the Pleasant View Mennonite Church in North Lawrence for seven years. Along with studies at Fuller beginning in 1974, he assisted on the ministerial staff at the Seventh Street Mennonite Church in Upland, California. From 1977 to 1980, he was pastor of the Santa Ana Church of the Brethren in California.

He has written *Divorce and the Faithful Church* (Herald Press, 1978) and a study course entitled "Spiritual Gifts and Ministries in the Church," with student manual and leaders guide.

Bontrager and his wife, Edie Shirk Bontrager, are the parents of two teenage daughters, Andrea and Michele.

95

# Coauthor

Nathan D. Showalter was born into a church planter's family and grew up in the Appalachian foothills of Kentucky among newly planted Mennonite churches. After college, he spent three years directing the music program of a fast-growing Baptist church in Nairobi, Kenya, whose international membership included persons from every part of Kenya as well as from four continents.

After returning to the States, Showalter graduated from the Fuller (Cal.) and Lancaster (Pa.) seminaries. For five years he was the associate pastor of the Mount Joy (Pa.) Mennonite Church. During that time he was director of Church Growth Training with the Mennonite mission office in Salunga, Pa., and helped to launch a church planting program that has resulted in more than fifty new congregations to date.

Later, while pursuing doctoral studies at Harvard, Showalter pioneered with Art McPhee a new Mennonite congregation in Boston, Mass.

He is currently helping to start a new church in Pasadena, California, and serves as assistant to the president with World Vision International, an organization that partners in evangelism and development work in more than 80 countries.

Showalter lives in southern California.